REVOLUTION
— on Our —
KNEES

30 Days of Prayer for Neighbors and Nations

DAVID & KIM BUTTS

PRAYERSHOP
PUBLISHING

TERRE HAUTE, INDIANA

Host a **Restoration Revolution Prayer Weekend**. Kick off your 30 days of prayer with a special event where Harvest Prayer Ministries' teachers encourage and challenge your congregation toward deeper levels of prayer. Contact Dave Butts at dave@harvestprayer.com, or go to www.harvestprayer.com and click on Teaching for information.

PrayerShop Publishing is the publishing arm of Harvest Prayer Ministries and the Church Prayer Leaders Network. Harvest Prayer Ministries exists to equip the local church to become a house of prayer for all nations, releasing God's power for revival and finishing the task of world evangelization. Its online prayer store, www.prayershop.org, has more than 600 prayer resources available for purchase.

© 2010 by Harvest Prayer Ministries

ISBN: 978-1-935012-16-0

1 2 3 4 5 6 7 8 9 10 | 2012 2011 2010

INTRODUCTION

Most revolutions don't begin with people seeking God on their knees. Revolution usually implies rebellion or uprising. However, *transformation* is a synonym for revolution. And that is the theme of this devotional. When God's people begin to pray, they align themselves with the intentions of His heart. Then transformation happens—transformation within us, but also in the lives of lost people as they are drawn to Jesus in response to our prayers.

Missions experts from all over the world now readily acknowledge that the most effective strategy for finishing the task of world evangelization is the power of God released through prayer. God Himself chose that way to accomplish His plans and purposes upon the earth. Unleashing God's power for the completion of the Great Commission is one of His primary purposes for the gift of prayer.

As believers we know that the fulfillment of His plan has not yet been accomplished. Why? Because many Christians do not feel a burden to intercede on behalf of lost people. In the lives of a lot of believers today, most prayers are centered upon our own personal needs and concerns for those close to us. We have not fully realized that we must lift our sights to embrace the desires of God. He wants to bring the transformational life of His Son, Jesus Christ, into the lives of every man, woman and child on the earth. Don't misunderstand, God cares deeply about our needs and struggles; but He has His sights set on those who have not yet heard about Jesus, and on those who still need to decide to make Him Savior and Lord of their lives.

Revolution on Our Knees: 30 Days of Prayer for Neighbors and Nations is a 30-day devotional that will align our prayers with the plans and purposes of the Almighty God. Seeing the power of God flow in our churches begins with prayer. Loving people into His kingdom begins with prayer. A single mom in your neighborhood, an unreached people group in India, the government leaders in a nation closed to the gospel—all need the touch of Jesus Christ.

When God's people begin to seek Him through their prayers, intercession and thanksgiving on behalf of "everyone" as Paul stated in 1 Timothy 2:1-4, He is pleased, because He wants *all* people to be saved. In response to our prayers, leaders and workers will be raised up from among our own congregations, churches will be planted, and resources will be developed that will have far-reaching impact for the cause of Christ. When we pray, families will begin developing relationships with international students on college campuses, Christian business leaders will begin to feel compelled by God to give of their time, talent and resources to help poor people all over the world to have hope through self-sufficiency, and Bibleless people will see the Scriptures come to life in the languages of their hearts.

As you, your family, small group or church family take this 30-day intercessory journey, be very aware that God will meet you here. Take time to seek Him and to listen to His voice as He speaks into your hearts. The Living Word, Jesus Christ, and His kingdom purposes will be revealed to you through Scripture as you pray in the certainty that you are in the very center of the will of the Father. Take time to carefully consider the prayer points and to purposefully do as many of the "Take Action" steps as God leads you to do. Most of all, ask God to increase your faith for the fulfillment of the Great Commission in our day! This is a revolution worth giving one's life to and for as we seek the transformation of those moving from death to life! In the midst of this revolution, we will see our own lives transformed, our churches catch fire spiritually, and our passion for the lost increased by the power of the God who is mighty to save!

DAY 1

―――――――――――― ✦ ――――――――――――

SHINE, JESUS, SHINE

"Arise, shine, for your light has come, and the glory of the LORD rises

upon you. See, darkness covers the earth and thick darkness is over the

peoples, but the LORD rises upon you and his glory appears over you.

Nations will come to your light, and kings to the brightness of your dawn."

(ISAIAH 60:1-3)

PRAYER FOCUS: *Revival in the Church*

Isaiah gives us a wonderful picture of revival among the people of God, with the result being an amazing influx of people into the kingdom. Three powerful words: light, glory, and darkness, burn lasting images onto our minds. The scenario presented by Isaiah is of a world in darkness . . . cut off from the light of the Presence of God.

Then suddenly, a light begins to shine upon a group of God's people. Then another light. Many lights begin to shine in the night. The contrast to the darkness around them is astonishing!

The prophet makes it clear that the light is God's glory! The simplest way to understand the word glory is God's Presence. God is showing up in the midst of His people. The light and glory of His Presence is beginning to be manifest as His people wake up to His Presence right where they are. This is revival!

Look at the response of those who are in darkness. Light in the midst of darkness becomes a summons to those who are perishing. Nations begin to flock to the light. There is coming a great harvest! It comes not because of our excellent evangelistic programs, but because the Church has humbled itself before the Lord in repentance and prayer, crying out for His Presence to be made manifest in our lives.

ASK THE ALMIGHTY

Father, how I long for Your Presence in my life! For too long, I've been content with little commitment, little faith, and little joy. No longer! Lord, I want You! I can never be content with anything other than Your Presence. I want to be like Moses who said he wasn't going anywhere unless You went with him. Forgive me, Lord, for going places in my own strength and for my own purposes.

Lord, I ask for Your light and Your glory to come upon Your people. May we shine like stars in the universe because of Your Presence! I long to see Your Light shine through believers in a way that will attract those living in darkness. Awaken Your people, O Lord, that the nations may see You, living in us.

PRAYER POINTS

- **Ask God** to pour out a spirit of revival upon the Church.
- **Ask God** to bring a spirit of repentance into your life, so that you might walk in humility before Him.
- **Ask God** to create in your life and in the life of your congregation a sense of desperation for God's Presence.
- **Ask God** to begin a work of holiness in the lives of believers that creates a dramatic contrast to the darkness that surrounds us.

TAKE ACTION

Recognizing our complete dependence upon God, consider gathering your family or a group of like-minded believers to fast and pray for God to pour out a corporate revival upon each of you personally, upon your church, the Church universal, and upon the nations. Focus on repentance and seeking the Lord's Presence. If you sense God is calling your church to do something corporately, talk with your pastor or church leadership.

DAY 2

———————————— ✦ ————————————

Know that He Is God

"Be still, and know that I am God; I will be exalted among the nations, I will be exalted in the earth." (Psalm 46:10)

Prayer Focus: *Exalting Christ among the Nations*

One Easter Sunday, flags from many nations, along with beautiful banners stating different names of God, were carried around our church to a beautiful worship song called *Hallelujah to the Lamb* written by Don Moen and Debbye Graafsma. The lyrics spoke of exalting the Lord Jesus among the nations. It was incredibly powerful and our sanctuary was filled with praise, applause, and acclamations to the King of Kings and Lord of Lords! We celebrated the risen Christ with joy and enthusiasm, recognizing that on this day, millions of believers from every tongue, tribe and nation were doing the same!

When was the last time you exalted Christ? In the busyness of our culture, it is often difficult to remember to take time from our frantic pace and acknowledge the Presence of the One who will be exalted among the nations. When I am too busy to allow the love and mercy of God to wash over me, and when I am too distracted to be aware of His majesty and power, my life is out of sync with my Savior!

Today, take time to remember the thrill of the Resurrection! He is Risen! Not just on Easter, but every day! Be still and know that He is God! He is alive and living in us! Exalt His Name in your life, your home, your church, and your nation! Give praise to the Lamb of God!

Ask the Almighty

Lamb of God, forgive my forgetful, ungrateful ways! Draw me close to Your heart in this moment. May I never release the awareness of Your Presence even in my busiest seasons of life. I exalt You, Lord Jesus! May every tribe, tongue and nation on earth bow before You in adoration and joyous praise! Help my life to be a celebration that honors what You have done to redeem Your people! Hallelujah to the Risen Christ, the resurrected Lamb of God!

Prayer Points

- **Ask God** to make you continually aware of His Presence, no matter how busy or hectic your life seems to be today.
- **Ask God** to help you find quiet moments just to be still and remember that He is your God, the One who is to be exalted in all the earth!
- **Ask God** to fill you with joy even in the midst of struggle and difficulty as a testimony to His power at work within you.
- **Ask God** to show you how to proclaim Him to others.
- **Ask God** to show you how your life is intended to exalt God in your family, church, neighborhood . . . and before the nations of the world.

TAKE ACTION

Make a list of the nations and people groups represented by the missionaries supported by your family and/or your church. Find pictures or maps to represent each, if you can. Place your hand on each picture or map and declare in faith that Christ will be exalted in the lives of these people and nations!

DAY 3

———————— ✦ ————————

WHAT'S YOUR NAME?

"And as he taught them, he said, 'Is it not written: "My house will be called a house of prayer for all nations?" But you have made it a den of robbers.'" (MARK 11:17)

PRAYER FOCUS: *The Church as a House of Prayer*

In three of the four gospels, Jesus quotes His Father from Isaiah 56:7. Such repetition makes this something of great importance to us, as it deals with the nature of the people of God. God's original house, the great temple in Jerusalem, is gone. But He still has a house. The Bible tells us that *we* have become the dwelling place of God, the temple of the Holy Spirit. That's true of us as individual believers, but also true of God's people as a whole, according to Paul.

Ownership clearly implies the right to name a house. God could have named us a house of Bible study . . . or a house of evangelism . . . or a house of fellowship. All are worthy names, but not what God has chosen to name us. God says we are to be called a House of Prayer for all nations.

Are you living up to your name? For an individual, being a house of prayer means more than having devotions in the morning. Prayer becomes an integral part of who you are. For a church, it doesn't mean tacking on a prayer meeting to an already busy schedule. It means prayer permeates every aspect of congregational life as prayer becomes the heart of who we are as the people of God.

ASK THE ALMIGHTY

Lord God, I am humbled that You have called me, my family and my church to be a house of prayer. In Your plan, that means we are a place and a people of Your power being poured out to bring lasting change. Please show me how to move consistently forward in my understanding and practice of prayer. Forgive me for my past prayerlessness. I turn to You, longing to experience a richer intimacy in prayer, and from that, have a greater understanding of how You would have me pray Your will. I look forward to the day when all of Your people humbly seek Your face. Help me Lord, to learn how to become a house of prayer for all nations!

PRAYER POINTS

- **Ask God** to make you as an individual, a house of prayer.
- **Ask God** to make your family members and your home a house of prayer.
- **Ask God** to make your congregation a house of prayer.
- **Ask God** to create a hunger within your church leadership for a greater intimacy with Jesus.
- **Ask God** to give your church leaders great wisdom in leading the church in prayer.

TAKE ACTION

Set up a small area of your home as a place of prayer, maybe just a corner or a favorite chair. If your church does not have a special room set aside for prayer, ask your church leadership for permission to create a place of prayer for your congregation.

DAY 4

AND THEN THE END WILL COME!

"This is what was spoken by the prophet Joel: 'In the last days, God says, I will pour out my Spirit on all people. Your sons and daughters will prophesy, your young men will see visions, your old men will dream dreams. Even on my servants, both men and women, I will pour out my Spirit in those days, and they will prophesy. I will show wonders in the heaven above and signs on the earth below, blood and fire and billows of smoke. The sun will be turned to darkness and the moon to blood before the coming of the great and glorious day of the Lord. And everyone who calls on the name of the Lord will be saved.'" (ACTS 2:16-21)

PRAYER FOCUS: *Spirit-filled Evangelism*

The audience on Pentecost was trying to make sense of the confusing scene unfolding before their eyes. Men were speaking of spiritual matters and everyone else was hearing them in their own heart language. Some illogically thought these speakers must be drunk. But Peter quoted from Joel 2 to show what was really taking place. This was the prophesied outpouring of the Holy Spirit that must come at the beginning of the last great epoch of mankind before the Lord Himself comes to rule over the planet.

It is understandable that almost 2,000 years later we find ourselves focusing on the phrases Joel used to describe what was to happen: prophecy, visions, dreams, signs and wonders, blood and fire, and billows of smoke. But to spend much time on these things is to miss the purpose of this great outpouring. Joel's purpose is made clear in Acts 2:21: "and everyone who calls on the name of the Lord will be saved."

The Spirit was poured out on Pentecost to open wide the gates of salvation. Believers in Jesus, not just that day, but throughout history, would be empowered through the Spirit to be witnesses. 3,000 were added to their number that day through the work of the Spirit in the lives of the believers. Nothing has changed in the plans of God. As Spirit-filled believers begin to speak of Jesus, the Lord will add to their number those who are being saved.

ASK THE ALMIGHTY

Lion of Judah, how I desperately need the power of Your Holy Spirit in my life today. I have tried to do Your work in my own strength and power and have failed. I need You! Help me to embrace the work of the Holy Spirit in my life. Lord, I long to see the kind of response that occurred on the Day of Pentecost in our churches today. May I turn from human methods and techniques and commit to seek You in Your power and glory. Come Holy Spirit!

PRAYER POINTS

- **Ask God** to pour out His Spirit upon you today.
- **Ask God** to come in power in your congregation.
- **Ask God** for a new Pentecost that ignites evangelism as it did in the book of Acts.
- **Ask God** to show you how the Holy Spirit is involved in spreading the gospel through your life.
- **Ask God** to awaken your church to the realization that we are living in the days of the open gates of salvation.

TAKE ACTION

Make a list of the things you have been trying to do for God in your own strength. What would happen if the Spirit empowered each of these things? Dream big with God and re-imagine your list.

DAY 5

UNLEASHING THE AUTHORITY OF HEAVEN

"Then Jesus came to them and said, 'All authority in heaven and on earth has been given to me. Therefore go and make disciples of all nations, baptizing them in the name of the Father and of the Son and of the Holy Spirit, and teaching them to obey everything I have commanded you. And surely I am with you always, to the very end of the age.'" (MATTHEW 28:18-20)

PRAYER FOCUS: *Our Commission*

Our youngest son is a policeman in our hometown. We're very proud of him and the fact that he serves our community. Every summer, he volunteers for the bike patrol, which gives him a better opportunity to interact with people. He told us that, because his bicycle has police lights and a siren, he is able to pull cars over, just as the patrol cars do. Now, every car on the road could outrun a policeman on a bicycle, but almost every car pulls over to the side of the road when the siren and lights come on. Why?

It's a matter of authority. Those lights, that bicycle, and our son in his police uniform, represent the authority of the law and our local government. Authentic authority allows you to do so much more than what you are able to do as an individual.

Who of us has within ourselves the ability to go to all nations and change cultures and transform lives? Yet, because all authority in heaven and earth has been given to Jesus, we are able to go in that authority and make a real difference . . . even if we're going by bicycle.

We love the last part of the Great Commission, where Jesus assures us of His Presence with us. Could it be that His Presence is directly tied to our going in obedience to His command? We believe this is so because He promises that if we do what He commands, He will be with us always . . . to the very end of the age!

ASK THE ALMIGHTY

Lord Jesus, I am in awe of this amazing command to go into all the world. I feel so small and insignificant; yet, You have said that with Your authority behind me, I am able to accomplish amazing things for the sake of Your kingdom. You will never leave or forsake me, for Your promise is to be with me to the very end of the age. I would be completely overwhelmed by this task without knowing that You will direct my steps and keep Your promises. Help me to embrace this Great Commission and to obediently fulfill whatever kingdom plans and purposes You set before me.

PRAYER POINTS

- **Ask God** to stir the Church to obedience regarding the Great Commission.
- **Ask God** to show you your part in fulfilling this command of Jesus.
- **Ask God** to help you to begin to understand the authority you have in Him as you follow His commands.
- **Ask God** to show you how you can begin to simplify your life so you are better able to go or give as He directs.

TAKE ACTION

Begin a "Prayer for the World" notebook or journal. Write at least one prayer for the world each day. Gather information on missionaries or unreached people groups that you can pray for.

DAY 6

LOOK UP AND SEE

"For the earth will be filled with the knowledge of the glory of the LORD,

as the waters cover the sea." (HABAKKUK 2:14)

PRAYER FOCUS: *Vision for the Church*

It is very easy in the midst of the difficulties and trials of everyday life, to lose our vision. Sometimes we slip into survival mode: "I just want to make it through today without messing up too much." Other times, we begin to develop a maintenance philosophy for the Church and our part in it. If we can just maintain where we've been, we'll be successful.

The pressures of everyday living seem to make fresh vision for the future a commodity we can't afford. We ask, "How can we possibly begin to dream of more, when we aren't doing very well with what we currently have?" And so we drift back into the weariness of plodding forward in our Christian lives, with our eyes firmly fixed on the ground in front of us so we don't stumble.

The prophet Habakkuk virtually grabs our heads and jerks us upward. "Look, can't you see?" he asks. "There is something on the horizon that is so huge that you won't be able to miss it," is the real message of Habakkuk. The prophetic Word from God is that there is coming a day when the knowledge of the glory (Presence) of God will be experienced on planet Earth. That shakes us to our core. Things will not always be as they have been. It is time for a fresh vision among the people of God! It is time to pray for the fulfillment of His Word.

Ask the Almighty

Lord, thank You for giving me this fresh vision from Habakkuk. I long for the day when the earth will know Your Presence by experience. Help me to live for that! Pour out Your Spirit upon me so that I may pray and live in a way that hastens that day. Forgive me Lord, for sometimes living a mediocre life that fails to take into account what You are longing to do in and around me. Give me fresh vision. Help me to see with the eyes of my heart what is on Your heart to do in and through me.

Prayer Points:

- **Ask God** to give you the spiritual eyes to see what He is doing in the world today.
- **Ask God** to give you personally, fresh vision of His purposes at work within you.
- **Ask God** to give the members of your congregation new insight into their purpose and where they fit in with what God is doing today.
- **Ask God** to fulfill in our day this prophetic word, that the glory of the Lord would cover the earth, as the waters cover the sea.

TAKE ACTION

Try dreaming a big dream. Is there something you have always wanted to do for God, but you haven't felt the time was right? Write it down and prayerfully commit it to the Lord to be accomplished in His timing and in His strength. Tell your dream to someone who will hold you accountable and who will help you to move forward as God leads.

DAY 7

———————— ⊕ ————————

ORDINARY PEOPLE

"Do everything without complaining or arguing, so that you may become blameless and pure, children of God without fault in a crooked and depraved generation, in which you shine like stars in the universe as you hold out the word of life—in order that I may boast on the day of Christ that I did not run or labor for nothing." (PHILIPPIANS 2:14-16)

PRAYER FOCUS: *Raising Up Leaders*

The Bible is a great book on leadership. It is filled with stories of very ordinary people whom God turns into leaders as they keep their eyes on Him and follow in His ways. Poor stuttering Moses, off in exile in the desert for murder, becomes the great lawgiver and deliverer of his people. Timid Gideon, hiding in a hole in the ground from his enemies, leads Israel to throw off the yoke of its oppressors. Saul, the legalistic persecutor of Christians, is transformed into Paul, the great apostle of grace.

In every church, in every nation, God is raising up leaders today. They are ordinary people, men and women just like us, who will hold out the word of life to a world that desperately needs it. Paul's letter to the Philippians gives great direction to those who are moving toward becoming spiritual leaders, commanding them to do everything without complaining or arguing, eagerly desiring to live blameless and pure lives. The result? Christians whose lives begin to shine like stars in the universe as they hold out the word of life. These are the kind of leaders the world is waiting to follow!

Ask the Almighty

Abba Father, please raise up leaders in the Body of Christ. How we need those who will live godly lives, serving as examples to Your people. Bless our Bible colleges, seminaries, and campus ministries as they train and equip young people for ministry and leadership. Pour out a spirit of prayer upon our emerging leaders, so that they would lead from a place of intimacy with You. Help our churches to be places that identify and set apart those called to leadership. Please raise up godly mentors for younger leaders, so that their paths would be made clearer by the example of those who have walked with You for many years.

Prayer Points

- **Ask God** to pour out a spirit of peace and joy upon you so that you will not be tempted to complain or argue.
- **Ask God** to raise up leaders from within your congregation who will shine like stars as they offer up the word of life to the lost.
- **Ask God** to strengthen college students in your congregation through campus ministries and godly instruction so that they will learn to lead from a place of deepest intimacy with Christ.
- **Ask God** to help you identify and nurture strong leaders within your congregation who have a deep desire to minister to lost people.

TAKE ACTION

Write letters of encouragement to young leaders from your congregation who are in Bible college, seminary or involved in a campus ministry on a secular college or university campus. Pray for them faithfully.

DAY 8

REMEMBER, TURN, BOW DOWN

"All the ends of the earth will remember and turn to the LORD, and all the families of the nations will bow down before him, for dominion belongs to the LORD and he rules over the nations." (PSALM 22:27-28)

PRAYER FOCUS: *The Nations*

It's frustrating to watch the news and see how the nations regularly ignore the Lord. Virtually all governments operate as though there is no God in heaven Who is Maker of all things and Ruler of the nations. Because of this rebellious attitude, humankind finds itself increasingly mired in unsolvable situations that threaten all of human existence.

It would be easy to lose hope if we did not have God's eternal Word as a sure promise. There is coming a day when the nations will: 1) remember, 2) turn, 3) bow down. The task of those who love God and already bow before Him in worship, is to continue to live in ways that honor the Lord and point people to Him.

The psalmist says that "the ends of the earth will remember." It's a fascinating use of words. Deep within all humankind lies a spiritual memory of our Creator. It may have been repressed, argued against, or legislated out of experience. The task of God's people, however, is to continually call the nations to remember Him, turn to Him and bow down in worship before Him.

God is waiting for the nations to remember, turn and worship. Our confidence in the midst of the trials of this world, is that there will come a day when the Lord will rule the nations.

Ask the Almighty

Father, the nations are in an uproar because they have turned their backs on You. Forgive us for looking to men for answers when the only answer is in You. Lord, I'm eager for the day when all the ends of the earth will remember and turn to You. What a time of magnificent worship that will be! I pray for the leaders of nations today, that they will remember You and turn. I pray that the Church would persevere in its task of declaring Your Name to all the families of the nations.

Prayer Points

- **Ask God** to touch the hearts of godless leaders who govern nations without His wisdom.
- **Ask God** for the hearts of people who have turned their backs on Him –that they would remember their Creator.
- **Ask God** for leaders and nations to turn away from sin and godless activity.
- **Ask God** to show Himself powerful in the midst of the nations so that lost peoples will bow down and worship Him alone.

TAKE ACTION

Choose a nation with a godless leader. Learn all you can about this person and his or her nation. Find a picture, if possible, and a map of the nation to put in your Bible or prayer closet so that you will remember to pray, using the prayer points above as a starting place.

DAY 9

BEAUTIFUL FEET

"And how can they preach unless they are sent? As it is written, 'How beautiful are the feet of those who bring good news.'" (ROMANS 10:15)

PRAYER FOCUS: *Releasing Kingdom Resources*

I (Kim) often long to be materially wealthy enough to provide for the needs of every missionary I know who has been called to go into all the world! So much valuable time is needed to raise support when a missionary could instead be preaching the gospel in a village in Africa, or working on a new Bible translation project for a Scripture-less people group in Asia. Even when we are not, our God is wealthy enough to provide! His resources are inexhaustible . . . but we must *ask* Him!

We need to become a people of prayer, asking the Lord of the Harvest to provide for these workers, recognizing that He may choose to use us, even if such obedience stretches our faith! Our hearts must be revived by the Holy Spirit so that we truly care deeply for the lost! Robert Hall Glover stated, "A mighty spiritual revival in the Church is the fundamental need of the hour; it is the only thing that will avail. . . . When revival comes the problems of missionary recruits and missionary support will be solved."

The eternal destiny for millions is dependent upon God's people crying out to Him! When revival comes, our hearts will be filled with great faith, and love will compel us to realize our part in providing for the beautiful feet of those who bring good news!

ASK THE ALMIGHTY

Jehovah Jireh, Your resources are inexhaustible, and Your faithfulness is unmatched! Help me to trust that You can use me, my family and my church to do incredible things for Your kingdom. Teach me to believe that You are able to provide just what is needed for those who are physically on the front lines of the battle for the souls of the lost! Help me to obediently respond in faith to the needs You place upon my heart. Revive me today! Awaken my soul to the voices of the lost crying out for the One they do not yet know. Deepen my passion to respond to the desperate needs of the widows and orphans, the poor and oppressed, and those who are imprisoned or marginalized by society. Put me on the spiritual front lines as a prayer warrior for the sake of Your kingdom now and forever!

PRAYER POINTS

- **Ask God** for a spirit of prayer (Zechariah 12:10) to come upon you, your family and your church.
- **Ask God** to pour out greater faith into your life and into the life of your church to believe He is able to use you to provide for the needs of at least one missionary family or missions organization.
- **Ask God** to show you, your family, small group or church how to provide for the spiritual and financial needs of missionaries associated with your church who are currently raising support to fulfill the call of God upon their lives.

TAKE ACTION

Spend some time sitting quietly before the Lord. What missionary, missionary family or mission group (Bible translation, medical mission, disaster relief, Bible College or university, literature production, technology, etc.) has He placed upon your heart? Step out in faith to meet a need and be a blessing. Then, expect to see God work through you as He pours out His abundant provision to meet your every need. See if He will not infect you with the joy and excitement of giving toward the advancement of His kingdom on this earth!

DAY 10

EVEN JESUS HAD TO ASK

"I will proclaim the decree of the LORD: He said to me, 'You are my Son; today I have become your Father. Ask of me, and I will make the nations your inheritance, the ends of the earth your possession.'" (PSALM 2:7–8)

PRAYER FOCUS: *That Jesus Would Receive His Inheritance*

This amazing passage of Scripture allows us to listen in on a conversation between God the Father and Jesus the Son. In a sense, the Father is saying, "Son, you will soon take on human flesh and live on planet Earth. Because of that, your inheritance will be the whole planet; every nation will be yours. But Son, because you will be fully human, you will have the same constraints that they have. This means that in order for you to receive from Me, you must ask. Even you, Son, must pray."

When the believers in the Jerusalem church were ordered by the authorities to stop preaching in the name of Jesus (Acts 4), they began to pray Psalm 2 back to God in response. They understood that for Jesus to receive His inheritance of all nations, they had to continue preaching the gospel, in spite of the orders given by the rulers. God's Word formed the basis of their prayer, and gave boldness to their preaching.

Today, Jesus has not yet fully received His inheritance. The nations must still hear. The ends of the earth have yet to be fully reached. It is time for us to join with Jesus, fervently asking for Him to receive all that the Father desires to give Him—the nations of the Earth!

ASK THE ALMIGHTY

Faithful Father, I thank You for the promise You have given to Jesus. I

23

thrill at the thought that one day, every knee shall bow and every tongue confess that Jesus Christ is Lord. Yet my responsibility is for today . . . that the ends of the earth, every nation, would come to hear the good news of Jesus. So today, as part of the Body of Christ, I come before You on behalf of the head of our Body and ask, "Father, please give Jesus His inheritance! May all nations come to know Him and adore Him." Please show me the part You have for me to play so that Jesus will receive all that You desire to give Him.

Prayer Points:

- **Ask God** to pour out a spirit of prayer upon every congregation.
- **Ask God** to help the Church begin to pray kingdom-focused prayers.
- **Ask God** to create within the Church a longing for Jesus to receive His inheritance.
- **Ask God** to raise up people, young and old, who will passionately go to the ends of the earth, in order to bring honor to Jesus and extend His kingdom.
- **Ask God** to stir the Church to give the resources necessary to finish the task of world evangelization in our day.

TAKE ACTION

Begin to ask the Lord for a nation or people group that you will have responsibility to pray for. Research that people group, perhaps using a resource like *Operation World* to find out what efforts are currently being made to reach them for Christ. Make a daily commitment to pray for that nation/people group, that they would soon become a part of the Lord's inheritance.

DAY 11

IT'S HARVEST TIME

"Then he said to his disciples, 'The harvest is plentiful but the workers are few. Ask the Lord of the harvest, therefore, to send out workers into his harvest field.'" (MATTHEW 9:37-38)

PRAYER FOCUS: *Laborers for the Harvest*

We love harvest time here in the Midwest. It is perhaps our favorite time of the year. When I (Dave) was preaching in a rural community, we saw firsthand that the harvest was the most critical time of a farmer's year. During those fall months, all the hard work from spring and summer was rewarded as the crops were brought in from the fields.

Harvest was a season of intense labor. Farmers knew they often had just a short period of time when the crops were ready and the weather would cooperate to allow them to bring in the harvest before harsh winter weather began. From early in the morning until late at night, farmers worked hard to assure a successful harvest.

There is another kind of harvest that is happening today: a harvest of souls. This spiritual harvest is a critical time, much as the fall harvest of crops. It too is a time of intense work in which the laborers cooperate with the Lord of the harvest to reap a harvest of souls.

Most church and mission groups can readily identify with Jesus' words that the laborers are few. What we need to emphasize here, however, is the Lord's command to pray. The first job of the church in the midst of harvest is to pray to the Lord of the harvest for an increase in workers. Are we obeying the Lord's command? Do we really believe that prayer will make a difference?

Ask the Almighty

Lord of the Harvest, I recognize that I live in a time of unprecedented openness and receptivity to the gospel message. You have opened more doors for Your people than we can go through. Would You awaken Your Church to the urgency of the hour? Teach me to pray this harvest prayer that Jesus commands me to pray. I ask Father, that You would give me Your heart for the harvest, so that I will always find this prayer for laborers to be on my lips.

Prayer Points

- **Ask God** to raise up laborers for the harvest.
- **Ask God** to bring to your remembrance this prayer on a regular basis.
- **Ask God** to call people from within your congregation to serve Him on the mission field or in church planting.
- **Ask God** to bring a new sense of urgency to you today regarding the harvest of souls.

TAKE ACTION

Discuss with members of your congregation how this "harvest prayer" can become a visible part of your church life. Could it be printed weekly in your bulletin, or perhaps painted on a wall in your church building? How can you make it front and center in your home?

DAY 12

SHAKING THE BUILDING

"After they prayed, the place where they were meeting was shaken. And they were all filled with the Holy Spirit and spoke the word of God boldly."

(ACTS 4:31)

PRAYER FOCUS: *Praying with Boldness*

The Jerusalem church was facing a crisis. The authorities had commanded the early believers not to preach anymore in the name of Jesus. What should they do? Their first response should be the response of every congregation of believers everywhere. They prayed. And oh, what a prayer!

These early Christians based their bold prayer on Psalm 2, acknowledging the hostility of the authorities to the Messiah, while affirming the Father's promise to the Son that He would receive all nations as His inheritance. They boldly asked God, not to step in to protect them, but to empower them to be witnesses in the face of opposition. They even asked the Lord to confirm their message with signs and wonders.

God's pleasure with their prayer is evident. He shook the building, filled them with the Holy Spirit (again!) and they immediately began to speak the word of God with boldness. Within weeks of this prayer meeting, even their enemies were saying that they had filled Jerusalem with their teaching (Acts 5:28).

When will the Church today pray such a prayer? In order to do so, we must be a people who are more interested in the kingdom of God than in our own comfort. We must be more concerned about the advancement of the cause of Christ, than about our retirement benefits or bank accounts. Are you willing to pray bold prayers that stir the heart of God to change circumstances and shake buildings?

Ask the Almighty

Mighty Father, teach us to pray like these early believers prayed. Help us to lay aside our fears and apprehensions and boldly pray and preach as they did. Lord, help us to not worry about opposition, but to pray in the face of it. Help us to not seek comfort and protection, so much as the proclamation of the message of Christ. Shake our churches again with Your power. Fill us again with Your Holy Spirit so that we may proclaim the word of God boldly.

Prayer Points

- **Ask God** to set you free from fear and timidity in spiritual matters.
- **Ask God** to pour out a spirit of bold prayer upon your congregation.
- **Ask God** to give you such a passion for the lost that you are willing to give up anything in order to see people saved.
- **Ask God** to teach you to pray His word with authority as these believers did.
- **Ask God** to help you to gather other believers to pray for those who do not know Jesus.

TAKE ACTION

The key to the amazing events in Jerusalem recorded in Acts 4 is a gathering of praying Christians. If you are not a part of a weekly prayer group that focuses on the purposes of God, join one. If none is available, start one. If you are a part of one, invite others to join you.

DAY 13

———————————— ⊕ ————————————

A CRISIS OF OBEDIENCE

*"While they were worshiping the Lord and fasting, the Holy Spirit said,
'Set apart for me Barnabas and Saul for the work to which I have called
them.' So after they had fasted and prayed, they placed their hands on them
and sent them off."* (ACTS 13:2-3)

PRAYER FOCUS: *Sending*

There is a story of a preacher who regularly challenged the young people in his church to come forward to dedicate their lives to missionary service. The church was supporting several of these youth who had chosen to respond when God placed a call to go into all the world upon their hearts. One Sunday, he preached a powerful message and gave yet another opportunity to those who felt called by God to missionary service. Yet, this day was different from all the others. This was the day that his own daughter walked up the aisle and stood before him, her eyes shining with excitement and joy. The preacher's heart plummeted to the floor as he watched her come, and anxiety sprung up in his throat. He had been prepared to send everyone else's sons and daughters, but had not considered the possibility that his own child might respond to God in this way. He faced a crisis of obedience in this moment when he felt both pride and fear welling up within him.

I don't know the rest of this story, but I hope that the preacher embraced his daughter's commitment, offering his encouragement and support as she answered the call of God upon her life.

His situation reminds us that when we ask the Lord of the harvest to send workers into His harvest field, we need to be serious about preparing ourselves, our children, our parents, etc. for the possibilities of what God may do in response. Perhaps God will call us to much prayer and fasting as part of such preparation so that He can reveal His plans and purposes to us.

Are you prepared to send those you love with your support and blessing? Will you step out in faith, committing yourself to send them out fully equipped spiritually as well as financially? Are you prepared to go if He is calling *you*?

ASK THE ALMIGHTY

Lord of the Harvest, prepare my heart in worship, prayer and fasting for all that You plan to use me for in the work of Your kingdom. I don't want to miss the opportunities you lay before me. Get me ready for the possibility that You may choose to call my children or grandchildren to places all over this world for Your sake. Help me to be willing to send those whom You have called by helping them to be prepared physically, spiritually, emotionally and financially. And, Father, prepare me to respond joyfully in whatever way You choose to use me.

PRAYER POINTS

- **Ask God** to teach you how to be a good sender as He shows you how to be involved in His purposes around the world.
- **Ask God** to make you generous with your time, talents and finances for the sake of His cause.
- **Ask God** to show you how to release those you love to His service, wherever it might take them.
- **Ask God** to make you willing to say, "Here am I, send me!"

TAKE ACTION

Set apart a day or two to fast and pray that God will raise up workers for His harvest field. Keep a journal as You listen to what the Spirit says. Invite others to fast and pray with you for the sake of those God calls from within your family and/or church. Be sensitive to whatever role the Father gives you in sending out the Barnabases and Sauls from your midst.

DAY 14

LIFE AS MISSION

"And this gospel of the kingdom will be preached in the whole world as a testimony to all nations, and then the end will come."
(MATTHEW 24:14)

PRAYER FOCUS: *The Second Coming*

The gospel is going to be preached to all nations. Jesus said so. If Jesus said so, then we believe it will happen. Sometime after the gospel has been preached to all nations, the end of all things will come. Evangelism is tied to the Second Coming of Christ. Sometimes we get caught up in the minutia. "What does it mean to preach the gospel to all nations?" "How soon after that will Jesus return?" On and on the questions come, until we find ourselves spending our time on the details instead of the main event.

The real question is, "Do we want to be a part of the fulfillment of Jesus' words?" If our answer is "yes," then we will find our lives caught up in the greatest of all adventures. Everything we do from this point on will revolve around who Jesus is and our desire for all people everywhere to know Him as we do. No longer will we see "missions" as a program within the church. Instead, we will see life as mission. Our prayer lives especially will begin to shift away from our own needs, and will focus on the completion of the Great Commission in our own day.

ASK THE ALMIGHTY

Holy Father, I can hardly wait for You to give the word for Jesus to return to planet earth. How I long to see Him face to face! But You have given us a task to do first. I ask You Lord, to pour out Your Spirit upon the Church to empower us to finish the task of world evangelization. Father, You are the only One who knows where the finish line really is. We seek in vain to try and figure out when and how we have completed what the Lord Jesus has given us to do. Set us free from such details, and help us to pull out all the stops in our desire to share Christ with everyone on the planet. Wake us up Lord. Let us be done with lesser things. Give us Your heart for those who are lost without Christ in this world. Come soon, Lord Jesus!

Prayer Points

- **Ask God** to give you compassion for those who are lost.
- **Ask God** to show you your own part in the task of world evangelization.
- **Ask God** to give you a greater passion for the return of Jesus.
- **Ask God** to unite your local congregation behind the mission of Jesus to the world.
- **Ask God** to raise up intercessors in your church who will pray daily for the completion of the task of world evangelization.

TAKE ACTION

Begin to pray the news! As you read news in the paper or on the internet, or as you listen to the radio or watch the television, begin to pray about the issues and situations that are presented. Ask God to bring His Presence into each life and situation. Instead of complaining about the news, or wishing it was different, make every news event a prayer event, calling upon God to get involved.

DAY 15

JESUS—THE MISSION AND THE MESSAGE

"'The Spirit of the Lord is on me, because he has anointed me to preach good news to the poor. He has sent me to proclaim freedom for the prisoners and recovery of sight for the blind, to release the oppressed, to proclaim the year of the Lord's favor.'" (LUKE 4:18-19)

PRAYER FOCUS: *Ministry that Makes a Difference*

Most churches today have mission statements that help them stay focused on the task ahead of them. Many individuals and families have also been encouraged to write a personal mission statement. This passage in Luke 4 can be considered to be Jesus' personal mission statement. As He read this passage, originally from Isaiah 61:1-2, in front of His hometown synagogue, He claimed it as His own mission in the world.

In a very real sense, Jesus Himself was both the mission and the message. To everyone, whether poor, blind, imprisoned or oppressed, the message was clear: God Himself was walking among the people of earth, and nothing would ever be the same! God's favor had come to the world through the person of His Son, Jesus.

The gospel message that we have is still the same. God walks among us. He dwells in His people as they live among broken, hurting people. He has come to make a difference. Jesus carries out His mission today through His people. Ultimately, His mission is yours. Are you living life on mission today?

Ask the Almighty

Awesome God, I thank You for the clarity in Your word concerning the mission of Jesus. There's nothing ambiguous in what You have said. Help me to take hold of Your mission and run with it. Give me Your compassion for those who are hurting or suffering. Please live out in my life the life of ministry that You demonstrated in the flesh. Increase my dependence upon the Spirit to proclaim the good news in everyday life.

Prayer Points

- **Ask God** to give you a stronger sense of mission and purpose in life.
- **Ask God** to show you each day who you are to minister to in the Name of Jesus.
- **Ask God** to sharpen the mission of your local church.
- **Ask God** to make you more sensitive to issues of injustice in life.
- **Ask God** to pour out His compassion for the hurting upon you.

TAKE ACTION

Write out a personal mission statement as you consider the life of Christ within you. Ask God to guide you in the process. Place your mission statement where you can easily see it each day as a reminder. Consider writing a mission statement as a couple or as a family if applicable.

DAY 16

CLARA'S PRAYERS

"No one can come to me unless the Father who sent me draws him, and I will raise him up at the last day." (JOHN 6:44)

PRAYER FOCUS: *Lost People*

This verse became very personal for me one winter, shortly after I (Kim) had given my life to Jesus. Clara, an older woman in my church, revealed that she had been praying for me daily for more than two years. She didn't really know me, but she knew that I needed to give my heart to Christ. The significance of that moment didn't hit me until I came face to face with John 6:44. Had God been drawing me while I was too busy to hear or pay attention? I could truthfully say that I had never known any other person who was interceding on my behalf. It made me ask, "What if she hadn't been praying for me?"

I believe that Clara's prayers allowed my heart to be open to the voice of the Holy Spirit. Because she cried out to God for my soul, I now have everlasting life. God was patiently wooing me, but in my ignorance and pride, I already believed I was going to heaven because I was a "good person." Clara prayed that I would bow my knee before the King of kings. As she did battle on my behalf, I began to soften my will before God, responding to His call to make His Son my Lord and Savior.

As God's people have gotten serious about the need to pray for the lost, neighbors, friends and families, and unreached peoples all over the planet are responding to Him. Even in nations where missionaries are not tolerated, people are having dreams and visions of Jesus. How is this possible apart from the Spirit of God drawing them to Himself in response to the prayers of God's people? Consider how many people are lost to the prince of darkness because no one has prayed that their lives would respond to a beckoning Father? I have no doubt that prayer is *the* front line strategy for missions. We may never know until heaven how many lives have been opened to receive Christ because of our prayers.

ASK THE ALMIGHTY

Spirit of the Living God, break my heart for lost people! Touch me in the deepest places of my soul with longing to be continually aware of those around me, and those around the world who have yet to come to You. Give me a burden to pray for their hearts to be opened so that they might respond as You draw them to Yourself. May I never make an assumption that someone else will pray when You have placed a person, a people group or a nation upon my heart. Use me, Father, to be the conduit that allows lost people to be drawn by You and to You.

PRAYER POINTS

- **Ask God** to soften your heart toward lost people so that you will be willing to pray for them as God leads.
- **Ask God** to give you a greater sense of urgency that the time is short so that you will not miss opportunities to pray for those whom God has placed on your heart.
- **Ask God** to give you a thankful heart for those who prayed you into the kingdom of heaven.
- **Ask God** to give you a burden to pray for lost neighbors and nations!

TAKE ACTION

Make a list of ten unsaved neighbors, friends or family members. Commit to praying for them daily, or at least regularly. Pray expectantly and with faith in God's ability to draw them to Himself. Celebrate whenever one of these precious people comes to Christ.

DAY 17

THE CHURCH GOES GLOCAL

"He came and preached peace to you who were far away and peace to those who were near." (EPHESIANS 2:17)

PRAYER FOCUS: *Neighbors and Nations*

Some Christians get so excited about global missions that they forget all about their neighbors at home. Other Christians are so focused on their neighbors that they don't think they have anything to give for the cause of world missions. The issue, in God's eyes, is not one or the other, but global *and* local evangelism. Some use the term "glocal" to describe this unified (and biblical) approach.

Jesus certainly viewed His ministry in this way. Though His first focus was on the Jewish people, he called them to fulfill their Abrahamic role of being a blessing to all nations by going to all peoples with the gospel. In this way, the gospel would tear down the barriers between Jew and Gentile and make one new man in Christ.

Paul described it to the church at Ephesus by saying that Jesus preached peace to those who were far away (the Gentiles), and He also preached peace to those who were near (the Jews). The peace of Christ brings peace between ethnic groups and nations, and brings those groups in peace to God.

Our calling from God is to be ministers of reconciliation (2 Corinthians 5:18), bringing the peace of Christ to those who are near us as well as to those who are far from us. Our prayer lives should reflect this dual emphasis. We should be praying for neighbors as well as nations.

Ask the Almighty

Gracious Father, Your love for all mankind is astonishing. Though You certainly deal with nations and people groups in different ways, Your love always shines through. I'm grateful for Your love in my own life. Help me to demonstrate this love in what I do and say, and especially in how I pray. May my prayers reflect Your love for those who are in my neighborhood, as well as for those who are on the other side of the planet.

Prayer Points

- **Ask God** to give you a great awareness of His love for you.
- **Ask God** to help you pray for nations in a way that reflects His love for them.
- **Ask God** to make you a bearer of His peace to everyone you encounter.
- **Ask God** to help your congregation stay balanced in its outreach, with work focused on both local and foreign evangelism.

TAKE ACTION

Choose one domestic mission and one foreign mission supported by your church that you do not already have some kind of connection with. Ask God to show you how to minister to these missionaries through letters of encouragement, prayer support and perhaps special financial gifts. Get others to join you.

DAY 18

TOOLS IN THE HANDS OF A MIGHTY GOD

"May God be gracious to us and bless us and make his face shine upon us, that your ways may be known on earth, your salvation among all nations. May the peoples praise you, O God; may all the peoples praise you. May the nations be glad and sing for joy, for you rule the peoples justly and guide the nations of the earth. May the peoples praise you, O God; may all the peoples praise you. Then the land will yield its harvest, and God, our God, will bless us. God will bless us, and all the ends of the earth will fear him." (PSALM 67)

PRAYER FOCUS: *International Students*

Every year almost 700,000 international students flock to college campuses in the United States. They are far away from home, many for the first time, navigating a strange culture and attempting to take classes in a language different from the one that is most natural to them. Many of these students want to impact their nations in a significant way, but most are not Christians. These students are a huge untapped resource for the cause of Christ, but about 70 percent of them will never see the inside of a Christian home unless we reach out to them.

The reality of this situation is staggering when we consider that these potential kingdom workers already know the language, customs and layout of their own countries. Through hospitality and acts of love, our families and churches can become the hands and feet of Christ to them, bringing many into the Kingdom of Light! Then, by training them to reach their own nations for Jesus Christ, these young men and women can become incredible tools in the hands of a mighty God.

ASK THE ALMIGHTY

Gracious Lord, please give me a heart for the nations, for I long to see all the ends of the earth fear Your Name! Help me to see the big picture of how reaching out to one young student can change the world for Jesus! Let me be one of many in my church to seek to build relationships with young men and women from all over the world so that they might have an opportunity to see the living Christ in our homes! Teach me to stretch beyond what is comfortable to learn from and minister to these young students, so that they will see Jesus in me and know that I care about them.

PRAYER POINTS

- **Ask God** to give you, your family and your church a heart for the salvation of international students and begin to pray for those on the college or university campus nearest to your home.
- **Ask God** to show you and your church how you can build a bridge by reaching out to international students with the love of Christ.
- **Ask God** to bless the evangelistic efforts of campus ministries reaching out to these lost international students.
- **Ask God** to show your church how to train up Christian leaders in the midst of the international student community who will one day impact their own nations for Jesus.

TAKE ACTION

Consider inviting an international student to come to your home for a meal, or to spend a holiday with your family. Allow a relationship to build and grow so that God will use you to plant seeds or to lead the student to Jesus. Organize an "adopt an international student" movement at your church, encouraging and training individuals and families to pray for, care about and mentor these young men and women. Commit to praying for one or more international students by name.

DAY 19

———————— ✦ ————————

GOOD NEWS FOR A CAPTIVE WORLD

"About midnight Paul and Silas were praying and singing hymns to God, and the other prisoners were listening to them. Suddenly there was such a violent earthquake that the foundations of the prison were shaken. At once all the prison doors flew open, and everybody's chains came loose. The jailer woke up, and when he saw the prison doors open, he drew his sword and was about to kill himself because he thought the prisoners had escaped. But Paul shouted, 'Don't harm yourself! We are all here!'

"The jailer called for lights, rushed in and fell trembling before Paul and Silas. He then brought them out and asked, 'Sirs, what must I do to be saved?'

"They replied, 'Believe in the Lord Jesus, and you will be saved—you and your household.'" (ACTS 16:25-31)

PRAYER FOCUS: *Setting the Captives Free*

Who was the real captive in this dramatic story in Acts 16? Paul and Silas, as well as several others, were sitting behind prison doors, their feet fastened in stocks. However, they were singing and worshipping the Lord at midnight. When a violent earthquake shook the foundations of the prison, it was the jailer who became a captive of fear, ready to kill himself.

The Lord's intervention through an earthquake certainly set free those who had physical chains like Paul and Silas. But it was the presentation of the good news of Jesus that set the real captive free. A jailer who was ready to kill himself over his apparent failure to keep his captives, was himself set free as he encountered Christ though Paul and Silas.

This story, typically without the earthquake, has been re-enacted throughout history. Jesus sets men free. He said of Himself in John 8:36, "So if the Son sets you free, you will be free indeed." Free from sin and its eternal consequences, free from fear, and free from death itself. The gospel is indeed "good news" to those who are captive. The preaching of Christ is not of more rules and regulations, but freedom to all who desire to receive the gift of life in Christ Jesus.

ASK THE ALMIGHTY

Lord of Compassion, I thank You for setting me free from sin and death. I rejoice in this freedom! Help me to speak everywhere I go of Your love, grace, and power to set the captives free. I ask You to please bring Your saving grace into the lives of those around me who don't know You. May the Good News that sets the captives free, flow from every Christian church around the world.

PRAYER POINTS

- **Ask God** to free those in your church who are held captive by their sins.
- **Ask God** to give you life-giving words to speak over those who are being held in bondage to their sins by the enemy of our souls.
- **Ask God** to free you from anything that is keeping you from experiencing freedom in Christ.
- **Ask God** to set your congregation on fire in the power of the Holy Spirit so that lost people will be attracted to the life that burns within you.

TAKE ACTION

Look for ways to get involved with those who are in prison by volunteering with an existing prison ministry. Contact prison chaplains to see if your family, small group or church can bring Bibles and Christian literature to a local jail or an area prison.

DAY 20

———————— ✦ ————————

LANGUAGE OF THE HEART

"Devote yourselves to prayer, being watchful and thankful. And pray for us, too, that God may open a door for our message, so that we may proclaim the mystery of Christ, for which I am in chains. Pray that I may proclaim it clearly, as I should. Be wise in the way you act toward outsiders; make the most of every opportunity. Let your conversation be always full of grace, seasoned with salt, so that you may know how to answer everyone." (COLOSSIANS 4:2-6)

PRAYER FOCUS: *Preaching with Clarity*

We both remember teaching in Thailand several years ago, which required from one to three translators depending upon how many different language groups were represented in the room. Sometimes the translator would not have a word for what needed to be translated, so much discussion would ensue to get the right meaning. By then, what we wanted to relate lost much of its effect. Sometimes the process of translation was long and involved, or so fascinating that we would forget what we had just said when it was time to move on to the next statement.

The apostle Paul knew that he must be clear when presenting the gospel; otherwise, his message would not be received seriously. Likewise, every preacher sometimes struggles to make sure the message being preached is clear and relevant to those who are listening. We have heard many stories from those who have unwittingly used the wrong words while trying to impart a spiritual truth, only to have everyone begin to laugh, or get confused looks on their faces. Imagine the difficulty of trying to preach in the heart language of a group of people who desperately need to hear a clear presentation of the gospel. Paul's prayer requests certainly apply to many missionaries today!

ASK THE ALMIGHTY

Amazing Lord, I am in awe at Your creativity! You have crafted an amazing world filled with colorful people, who are vastly different from one another in language and culture. Into these lands You have called Christian workers, many who preach Your Word in a second language. Would You anoint these preachers for this crucial task, and help them to clearly proclaim the message of the gospel of Jesus Christ to the lost? Give them confidence that Your Holy Spirit will speak through them so that Your Name will be made famous in the smallest villages and the largest cities throughout the world!

PRAYER POINTS

As you think of missionaries you know who are preaching the gospel from God's Word and through their everyday lives:
- **Ask God** to open doors for them to preach the gospel to the lost.
- **Ask God** to smooth the process of language learning so that the mystery of Christ can be proclaimed!
- **Ask God** to prepare hearts of lost people to be open to hear the word of the Lord to them.
- **Ask God** to speak clearly through every message that is preached!
- **Ask God** to allow preachers to make the most of every opportunity.
- **Ask God** to fill preachers with the grace and wisdom necessary to answer questions and to have just the right words to speak in everyday conversations with people.

TAKE ACTION

Send a letter of encouragement to one or more missionary preachers you and/or your church supports. Share the passage from Colossians 4:2-6 and how you have been and will continue to pray for them. Additionally, consider writing a note of encouragement to your own preacher today!

DAY 21

FOOD THAT SATISFIES

"'My food,' said Jesus, 'is to do the will of him who sent me and to finish his work. Do you not say, "Four months more and then the harvest"? I tell you, open your eyes and look at the fields! They are ripe for harvest. Even now the reaper draws his wages, even now he harvests the crop for eternal life, so that the sower and the reaper may be glad together. Thus the saying "One sows and another reaps" is true. I sent you to reap what you have not worked for. Others have done the hard work, and you have reaped the benefits of their labor.'" (JOHN 4:34-38)

PRAYER FOCUS: *Doing the Will of God*

What are you eating? Food is necessary to give strength and to sustain life. When we eat the right foods, it helps keep our bodies functioning properly. Look what Jesus said is His food. What sustains Him and gives Him strength is His determination to do the will of His Father and to finish His work. He looks at the world as a great harvest field, with many souls ready to be brought into the kingdom.

When Jesus calls us into the harvest field of this world as a laborer alongside Him, He is not calling us to a job, but to a lifestyle. Our food, our sustenance, becomes the same as His. We look at our labor in the harvest not as a burden, but as our joy in doing the will of the Father.

The general teaching of the Bible is that enjoying food is good. Even the idea of fasting—giving up food for a period of prayer—implies we give up something good for something even better. Feasts are times of great joy in Scripture. Are you experiencing great joy as you eat the food Jesus is eating . . . and do the will of the Father? Working in the harvest fields alongside Jesus should be our great privilege and joy!

ASK THE ALMIGHTY

Oh Lord Jesus, how I thank You for the feast You have set before Your people. You have given us the food of finishing the work the Father has given us to do, and I am grateful. Help me, Lord, to see my labor in Your harvest fields from heaven's perspective. Give me open eyes to see the ripe fields before me. Empower me by Your Spirit to work in Your strength and might and not in my own. Give me the wisdom to tackle the section of the field that You have assigned me. Empower me so that I will not be overwhelmed by the immensity of the task. It is, after all, Your field and Your work. I'm thankful You grant me this great privilege of serving in Your fields with and alongside You.

PRAYER POINTS

- **Ask God** to give you greater joy as you serve Him.
- **Ask God** to help you to see your service to Him as food for your soul.
- **Ask God** to make clear to you the area of the harvest that you are to be involved in.
- **Ask God** to give your local congregation a greater sense of what it means to be co-laborers with God in the great harvest of souls.

TAKE ACTION

Prepare a meal of your favorite foods. Then, with family and friends, eat the meal together, making it a time of prayer and thanksgiving to God. Ask Him in the midst of the meal to give you as great a joy in doing His will as you are having at that time.

DAY 22

ARE YOU A WORLD CHANGER?

"For as the soil makes the sprout come up and a garden causes seeds to grow,

so the Sovereign LORD will make righteousness and praise spring up before

all nations." (ISAIAH 61:11)

PRAYER FOCUS: *Christian Media and Technology*

Our friend, Karen, began the Hollywood Prayer Network via email and the web several years ago. She is a Christian who has been living and working in this dark place, ceaselessly attempting to gather together believers to pray with and encourage one another. The network's purpose is to pray for the people, the projects and the powerful influence of the entertainment industry. HPN believes that "by mobilizing global prayer we can be a part of God's miraculous work of changing the spiritual climate of Hollywood, from the inside out."

Sherwood Baptist Church in Albany, GA has been changing the world for several years now by making movies like *Facing the Giants* and *Fireproof*. Its mission statement is to "touch the whole world with the whole word, motivated by a passion for Christ and compassion for all people."

Recently, a ministry was begun that uses the internet for evangelism. Online missionaries are seeing 1.4 million people a month to make first time decisions for Jesus Christ. They follow up with online Bible studies and connect these new believers with churches in their areas. The goal is to give every man, woman and child on the planet an opportunity to hear the good news of Jesus a minimum of ten times over the next ten years.

These are only three snapshots of what is happening all over the world to utilize media and technology for the cause of Christ. God gave great vision to people who had faith enough to trust His ability to work through them to do something so big that it could never be imagined apart from Him. He has used them to allow "righteousness and praise to spring up before all the nations." Is God calling you to stretch your faith to believe that He can use you to be a world changer too?

Ask the Almighty

Thank You, Father, for the people You have called to change the world through media and technology. I am awed by the myriad of possibilities to reach the lost! Show me how to use the internet in life-giving ways! Help me to support Christian films that not only draw people to the loveliness of Christ, but which can be used as a tool to finance additional missional work!

Prayer Points

- **Ask God** to help you see ways to utilize the internet for Christ.
- **Ask God** to free up finances so you can support Christian media (radio, television, films, etc.)
- **Ask God** to raise up young servants from your church who will work in media and technology to impact the hearts of a lost generation.
- **Ask God** to save the lost in Hollywood who are producing films and television shows that are dishonoring to Him, so that their testimonies and future work will have great impact for God's kingdom.

TAKE ACTION

If you are currently using the internet for social networking, ask God how you can begin to impact the lives of others in missional ways. Perhaps He will direct you to be an online missionary!

Notify your friends, family and church whenever a Christian film is showing in your area so they can support it! Be instrumental and intentional about seeking out films that honor Jesus in their message. Invite friends and neighbors to your home for dinner and a movie!

Join the Hollywood Prayer Network (www.hollywoodprayernetwork. org) and pray for those who have great influence for good or ill over the entire world.

DAY 23

---◍---

FROM JERUSALEM TO THE ENDS OF THE EARTH

"But you will receive power when the Holy Spirit comes on you; and you will be my witnesses in Jerusalem, and in all Judea and Samaria, and to the ends of the earth." (ACTS 1:8)

PRAYER FOCUS: *Witnessing in the Power of the Spirit*

The words Jesus spoke to the apostles just before ascending into heaven are inspiring, but not comforting. He gave them a vast vision of the kingdom of God that would go to the very ends of the earth. That's inspiring! However, the word Jesus used to describe how such a thing will happen is not reassuring. The vision will be fulfilled as the followers of Jesus become witnesses. The word used in the Greek text is *marturia* . . . the root for our word "martyr." It is not very reassuring to know that this work will be accomplished only as God's people lay down their lives as martyrs.

Jesus certainly doesn't mean that every Christian witness is going to die a martyr's death. Yet, the word demonstrates that to be a witness for Jesus is not just about what you do, but about who you are. The activity of witnessing through words is very important; however, being a living witness for Jesus, willing if need be to lay down our lives for the advancement of the kingdom, is essential.

This sort of radical lifestyle, which marked the lives of the early Christians, is possible only through the work of the Holy Spirit. When we speak of the power of the Spirit, our thoughts often go to miracles and healings, etc. Certainly those things are a part of what the Spirit does in and through believers. But the power spoken of in Acts 1:8 is to be a wit-

49

ness . . . to live a life that is so "sold out" for Jesus that we are ready to go and do whatever He asks . . . whatever the cost!

ASK THE ALMIGHTY

Gracious God, I ask you to fill me again with your Holy Spirit. Give me the power to live as Your witness. And Lord, what I'm asking for myself, I ask for my church. Empower us Lord, to be a people who live your message every day of our lives. I am thrilled by the vision of taking Your gospel to the very ends of the earth. Please pour that revelation into the hearts of everyone in my congregation. Help us to put feet to this vision as we live our lives for you.

PRAYER POINTS

- **Ask God** to empower you through His Holy Spirit.
- **Ask God** to pour out His Spirit upon your church and the Body of Christ worldwide.
- **Ask God** to help you to embrace the cost and to live out the life of a true witness.
- **Ask God** to help you to pray faithfully for the nations to come to Christ.
- **Ask God** to open new doors for sharing Christ with others.

TAKE ACTION

One of the simplest ways to share your faith is to tell someone else the story about how God has worked in your life. Write out your testimony—your story—and practice saying it so that you are prepared whenever anyone asks you to give reasons for your faith. If you have already written your testimony, but haven't shared it for awhile, dust it off and take a look at how God has been working in your life. Because God is so faithful, your testimony probably needs some updating!

DAY 24

THE JOB OF THE BRANCH

"Remain in me, and I will remain in you. No branch can bear fruit by itself; it must remain in the vine. Neither can you bear fruit unless you remain in me. I am the vine; you are the branches. If a man remains in me and I in him, he will bear much fruit; apart from me you can do nothing."
(JOHN 15:4-5)

PRAYER FOCUS: *Bearing Fruit for the Kingdom*

Recently, we had the opportunity to speak to the staff of a large missions organization in Michigan. While there, we were housed in an old home with lovely gardens. There was a magnificent grape arbor that stretched as a canopy over a long walkway on the grounds. As we strolled underneath it one afternoon, I (Kim) was reminded of this passage in John 15. There were large, full clusters of grapes hanging from sturdy branches that could be traced back to several huge vines rising out of the ground. It was apparent that without these vines, the branches could not produce the lovely fruit in front of us.

When teaching on this passage, we often ask people, "What is the job of the branch?" Most will quickly answer, "To bear fruit." Yet, Jesus clearly says that "no branch can bear fruit by itself; it must remain in the vine." Therefore, the true job of the branch is to stay attached to the vine. It is a good illustration for us all to recognize that apart from the power of the Holy Spirit, who keeps us attached to the Vine, Christ Jesus, we can do nothing. We are unable to bear fruit that lasts (John 15:16) unless we live, move and have our being in Him (Acts 17:28). It should be our focus as

Christ followers to go wherever the Vine goes, and to yield ourselves to whatever the Vine wishes to produce in and through us.

E. M. Bounds stated, "To be little with God is to be little for God." Prayer keeps us attached to the Vine as God brings His life to our efforts on behalf of His kingdom.

Ask the Almighty

Lord Jesus, thank You for the reminder that it is only in Your strength that anything I do will bear fruit for Your kingdom. Help me to be a person of prayer who is continually attached to the Vine. Keep me from striving to do things on my own, expecting to serve You, for my gifts and abilities flow from You alone. Pour into me a spirit of humility to submit myself to Your Lordship, and to give all credit for success to You. Fill me with joy because I am a lowly branch that functions only when the life-giving nutrients of the Vine flow through me. Apart from You, I can do nothing . . . but *with* You I can do all things.

Prayer Points

- **Ask God** to give you the humility to submit to staying attached to the Vine.
- **Ask God** to help you recognize when you are trying to live and serve in your own human strength.
- **Ask God** to remind you that apart from Him you can do nothing.
- **Ask God** to give you the strength to be faithful to all He has called You to be and do.
- **Ask God** to make you a fruitful servant for His kingdom work.

TAKE ACTION

Consider praying about offering yourself to be a mentor, encourager or prayer warrior for a young person in your church who has expressed an interest in serving God through missions, or who is currently serving. Be a loving reminder for this young person to stay attached to the Vine.

DAY 25

CALLED TO MACEDONIA

"During the night Paul had a vision of a man of Macedonia standing and begging him, 'Come over to Macedonia and help us.' After Paul had seen the vision, we got ready at once to leave for Macedonia, concluding that God had called us to preach the gospel to them." (ACTS 16:9-10)

PRAYER FOCUS: *Business as Mission**

The apostle Paul preached the gospel in every city, small village or country the Lord called him to. Because he did not wish to be a burden to the young churches being planted, and so that he might win over unbelievers, Paul often made tents to support his evangelistic work. Because of his example, there are thousands of tentmaking missionaries all over the world today.

In this passage, Paul was called to Macedonia by means of a vision. He and his companions, Silas and Timothy, were obedient to the leading of the Spirit, believing with the eyes of faith that they would see people respond to Jesus. God was faithful to connect them with the open heart of Lydia, a businesswoman sitting by a river outside of Philippi. She was "a dealer in purple cloth from the city of Thyatira," and also "a worshiper of God" (Acts 16:14). When Paul spoke the message of the gospel of Jesus Christ, she responded, along with other members of her household.

It would be interesting to know how Lydia's new faith in Christ transformed the way she did business. We do know that she opened her home

---

*Business as mission is about viable, sustainable and profitable businesses with a kingdom of God purpose, perspective and impact leading to transformation of people and societies spiritually, economically and socially, to the greater glory of God.—Wayne McGee

to Paul and his companions on at least two occasions. First, right after her baptism, and then right after Paul and Silas were released from prison. We can probably make the assumption that her new faith in Jesus impacted the way she conducted both her life and her business dealings, and that she was a witness for Christ by serving the poor and marginalized around her.

Today, more and more Christian business leaders are using their skills and contacts to serve Christ around the world. Business as mission opens up a whole new area of evangelistic opportunity as people and even entire communities without hope are trained and/or funded so that they can adequately provide for themselves and their families.

Ask the Almighty

Lord of All, thank You for the story of these two business people meeting as a result of the vision You gave to Paul. Because he chose to be obedient and eager to see souls won for Christ, he made a journey that resulted in many people giving their hearts to Jesus. Help me, my family and my church family to see the value of helping the poor and marginalized of the world to be able to support themselves. Raise up those in our midst who would give of their time and talent to share in business as mission endeavors. May many lost people, in their gratefulness to the provision of God, seek and find Jesus through the love of His people ministering in this important way.

Prayer Points
- **Ask God** to show you where your Macedonia might be.
- **Ask God** how you might utilize your business skills and/or knowledge in or for missions.
- **Ask God** to raise up businesspeople in your church who would be willing to use their gifts to help the cause of Christ on the mission field.
- **Ask God** how He wants to use your business or your place of work to be a blessing to others.

TAKE ACTION

Find out more information about business as mission and tentmaking by talking with or joining the missions team of your church. Learn about ways you can help or get involved in changing the lives of people all over the world.

DAY 26

————————— ⊕ —————————

SHARING THE HOSPITALITY OF GOD

"They devoted themselves to the apostles' teaching and to the fellowship, to the breaking of bread and to prayer. Everyone was filled with awe, and many wonders and miraculous signs were done by the apostles. All the believers were together and had everything in common. Selling their possessions and goods, they gave to anyone as he had need. Every day they continued to meet together in the temple courts. They broke bread in their homes and ate together with glad and sincere hearts, praising God and enjoying the favor of all the people. And the Lord added to their number daily those who were being saved." (ACTS 2:42-47)

PRAYER FOCUS: *Neighborhood Evangelism*

Every year we have a Christmas open house. Starting in October, we begin to make and freeze a large variety of cookies, candies, breads, etc. Besides friends and family, we also make a point to invite our neighbors. Since many don't come, we make plates of the left-over goodies to take around to those who live on our block. I remember the Chinese man who tried to take one cookie off the plate we were offering to him. He couldn't believe that the entire plate was just for him. He and his wife have attended our open house every year since then. Such a simple gesture, yet, it opened up opportunities for a Buddhist family to see the love of Jesus in us. When was the last time you allowed the loveliness of God to be demonstrated through your life to a lost person? Who are you inviting into your home or reaching out to experience the hospitality of Christ in you?

ASK THE ALMIGHTY

Loving Lord, Your very life extended the hospitality of God's grace to everyone. Teach me to love people in ways that allow them to be touched by You. May lost people see the love that Your people have for one another, and be attracted by and to the fellowship that believers in Christ share. Help me to stretch out my hand in neighborly love to those who live and work around me, for unbelievers will not see You in me if I don't reach out to them. Show me simple ways to love others so that they will want to know more about the One I love!

PRAYER POINTS

- **Ask God** to give you His extraordinary love for believers and unbelievers alike.
- **Ask God** to help you to obediently respond to the impulses of the Spirit to show kindness, care and concern for those who live and work near you.
- **Ask God** to show you how to extend hospitality to others in loving ways.
- **Ask God** to make your home a place of refuge and peace so that your friends and neighbors can sense the love of God there.

TAKE ACTION

Begin to prayerwalk your neighborhood, or, if you live in the country, do some drive-by praying of the homes in your area. Ask God to open the hearts of your neighbors to receive Christ. Write down anything the Spirit might say to you about the people and families whose homes you go by and respond in obedience.

Begin to extend the same hospitality to people in your neighborhood as you would to your friends and family. You can invite them to your home, share a batch of cookies, offer to pick up mail if someone is going on a trip, etc. There are many small and simple expressions of the hospitality of Christ that can be offered to others.

DAY 27

THE JUSTICE OF JESUS

"Here is my servant whom I have chosen, the one I love, in whom I delight;

I will put my Spirit on him, and he will proclaim justice to the nations.

He will not quarrel or cry out; no one will hear his voice in the streets. A

bruised reed he will not break, and a smoldering wick he will not snuff out,

till he leads justice to victory. In his name the nations will put their hope."

(MATTHEW 12:18-21)

PRAYER FOCUS: *Hope for the Nations*

Every second of every day, difficult and sometimes atrocious things are happening to people God loves all over the world. Children die of starvation or disease, babies are aborted, people are imprisoned unjustly, families become homeless, people lose jobs . . . the list is long and heartbreaking. In the midst of all of this devastation, Jesus Christ brings peace and hope to those who suffer. He mends broken lives and proclaims that justice will be lived out in the lives of His true followers for the sake of the nations. He promises eternal life, where every tear will be wiped away and what is broken will be restored to wholeness.

Jesus is the answer to oppression, to terrorism and to poverty. His life makes poor people feel wealthy, downtrodden people dance, and suffering people sing for joy. In the midst of our circumstances we are still able to give thanks to the One who has given us everlasting life. Our God walks us through the very shadow of the valley of death! The hope deposited within us may be the only hope some people will ever see or experience.

Christ has compelled us to follow Him and to serve in His cause. Our ministry is always to be the hands and feet of the Lord so that His Name is made famous throughout the earth. If we have truly set Christ apart as Lord in our hearts, we must always be prepared to give an answer to everyone who asks us to give the reason for the hope that we have (1 Peter 3:15). It is truly a hope for all the nations!

ASK THE ALMIGHTY

God of Hope, Jesus is the only hope for those who are poor, oppressed and suffering all over the world. His life in me is the gift I have to give others to help alleviate such situations. Teach me to be open to the voice of the Spirit as He makes me aware of the ways in which I can be used to extend hope to hopeless people. May I be Jesus with flesh for those who have yet to know how much they are loved and valued by Him. Use me to bring justice to the hurting and helpless in Jesus' Name.

PRAYER POINTS

- **Ask God** to receive your thanks for His faithfulness in your life, even when circumstances have been difficult or painful.
- **Ask God** to show you how you can be the hands and feet that meet the needs of those in unjust situations.
- **Ask God** to break your heart when you see injustice so that you will be compelled to pray and act.
- **Ask God** to remind you how He has acted on your behalf to make right a wrong. Give Him thanks and praise once again.

TAKE ACTION

Do you know of an unjust situation in your city, nation or another part of the world? First, begin to pray. What could you do to shine the light of Christ into that situation? If you cannot do anything physically, could you make phone calls or write letters? Could you make others aware of the situation who are able to have influence in bringing justice? God desires to work through the prayers and activity of His people. As you make yourself available to Him, He will work through you!

DAY 28

———————— ✦ ————————

THE DIVINE SOLUTION

"My prayer is not for them alone. I pray also for those who will believe in me through their message, that all of them may be one, Father, just as you are in me and I am in you. May they also be in us so that the world may believe that you have sent me. I have given them the glory that you gave me, that they may be one as we are one: I in them and you in me. May they be brought to complete unity to let the world know that you sent me and have loved them even as you have loved me." (JOHN 17:20-23)

PRAYER FOCUS: *Unity in the Body of Christ*

I (Dave) remember my amazement at listening to her prayer. *She knows Jesus!* was my thought. Since she was the representative of a denomination that was known for its theological liberalism, I wasn't expecting that from her, which was my mistake. It's so easy to place labels that divide Christian from Christian. Living in a world of literally thousands of associations, networks, fellowships of churches and denominations, the Body of Christ appears to be tragically fragmented.

Hope for healing, however, can be found in this prayer Jesus prays for unity. It doesn't take a trained theologian to see that Jesus was passionate about unity in His Body. His prayer reflects not only His desire, but perhaps also opens a way for the realization of this unity. Pray with Jesus! Pray with His passion that we all would be one in Him. There's no human solution to our divisions, but there *is* a Divine solution. We do not have to agree theologically with everyone, but we can agree to love one another and to form loving partnerships with one another on behalf of lost people!

As we begin to pray with Jesus around His great desire for unity, we will find our hearts lining up with His. Passion for unity will grow within us. Not unity in the sense of some big super-church that embraces everyone, but unity within the various tribes that make up the Body of Christ. A unity, not of structure, but of the heart and of purpose. Join with Jesus in praying for unity, and we'll be well on the way toward achieving His heart!

Ask the Almighty

Lord Jesus, I join my prayer to Your prayer for unity among those who follow You. Please give me that kind of passion for unity. Help me to live in a way that demonstrates Your love for my brothers and sisters in Christ. Lord, I plead with You to keep me from saying or doing anything that would create division within the Church. May we be brought to complete unity in order to demonstrate to a watching world that You, Lord, were sent by the Father to demonstrate His great love for us.

Prayer Points

- **Ask God** to give you a heart that longs for unity in your home and in your church.
- **Ask God** to pour out a spirit of unity within the hearts of believers in all of the churches of your city.
- **Ask God** to forgive you for making wrong assumptions about the spiritual condition of people, and ask Him to give you a heart filled with love for everyone.
- **Ask God** to show you the beauty of His body functioning in your own community.
- **Ask God** to show you how to encourage and foster the kind of unity that will attract unbelievers to Jesus.

TAKE ACTION

Volunteer to help with a community-wide prayer and/or evangelistic effort that honors God such as the National Day of Prayer, Global Day of Prayer, etc. Make an effort to get to know people from other churches in your area and appreciate the diversity of the Body of Christ.

DAY 29

FAITHFUL TO THE END

"However, I consider my life worth nothing to me, if only I may finish the race and complete the task the Lord Jesus has given me—the task of testifying to the gospel of God's grace." (ACTS 20:24)

PRAYER FOCUS: *Completing the Task*

It was an unusual Sunday afternoon at my (Dave's) old hometown church. The church was recognizing several women from the congregation who were stepping down after more than forty years of ministry in the Sunday school program of the church. Forty years on the frontlines of ministry! Forty years of providing Bible teaching and leadership to generations of children.

In our day, such persistence and endurance is often rare. We take on tasks for short-term, not willing to make a commitment for years at a time. We often start things, giving no thought to what it will take to actually finish.

Paul was passionate about finishing what he began. Whether you view it as a race or a task, he wanted to finish it well. The Church has been given the same task that Paul had been given—testifying to the gospel of God's grace. Whether we are living on the mission field, preaching in a local church, or serving in our own congregation, faithful service to the end is essential to completing the task. May we be the generation that sees the whole gospel go to the whole world through the patient endurance of those who have set their hand to the task and who will not quit.

ASK THE ALMIGHTY

King of Kings, the privilege of serving You is amazing. That You would entrust me with tasks that relate to Your eternal purposes, doing those things that help draw others to Jesus and encourage them in their faith, is beyond anything I could have imagined. Help me to be faithful. Give me perseverance. Help me to not grow weary in well-doing. And Lord, give me words of encouragement for others, so that they will also finish the race You have set before us.

PRAYER POINTS

- **Ask God** to give you a determined spirit to serve Him—a spirit that does not give up regardless of the obstacles.
- **Ask God** to pour out a spirit of perseverance upon your congregation.
- **Ask God** to keep before your eyes the task of testifying to the gospel of grace.
- **Ask God** to raise up encouragers in your congregation who will strengthen one another for lifelong ministry.

TAKE ACTION

Make a commitment personally, as a family, with your small group, or as a church, to provide prayer, encouragement and/or financial support for a church planting team. Don't quit until the church is firmly established.

DAY 30

THE WORLD WORSHIPS

"After this I looked and there before me was a great multitude that no one could count, from every nation, tribe, people and language, standing before the throne and in front of the Lamb. They were wearing white robes and were holding palm branches in their hands. And they cried out in a loud voice: 'Salvation belongs to our God, who sits on the throne, and to the Lamb.' All the angels were standing around the throne and around the elders and the four living creatures. They fell down on their faces before the throne and worshiped God, saying: 'Amen! Praise and glory and wisdom and thanks and honor and power and strength be to our God for ever and ever. Amen.'" (REVELATION 7:9-12)

PRAYER FOCUS: *Worship and Missions*

Tears were running down my face as I (Dave) joined with over 5,000 brothers and sisters, worshipping the Lord in a most amazing way. We were in Seoul, South Korea, for a major missions conference, with delegates from 200 nations, representing many languages and people groups. The worship leader had just announced the name of the old familiar hymn we were to sing, and then it happened. He said, "Each of you sing this in your own language." As thousands of voices began to sing, in hundreds of languages, my thoughts turned to Revelation 7 and the picture of multitudes worshipping before the throne of God and of the Lamb. I was experiencing worship in a way that was a taste of what was to come . . .

when believers "from every nation, tribe, people and language" would join together in worshipping the Lord.

John Piper's words stood out glaringly as I remembered this moment: "missions exists because worship does not." The eternal destiny of mankind is to worship before the Throne of God. Because many have chosen not to worship, missions is necessary. We must proclaim the glories of God in such a way that the nations are drawn to worship Him.

ASK THE ALMIGHTY

Majestic Father, I long for the day when I see You face to face, falling down before You in worship and adoration. It is hard for me to imagine the eternal joy that will be mine as one who is privileged to join with people from all nations and languages, worshipping before Your throne. Father, what I earnestly desire now is to be a part of helping many others become worshippers. Show me ways to point others to Jesus, so that they too may experience the joy of worshipping You.

PRAYER POINTS

- **Ask God** to draw you near to Him in wonderful times of worship.
- **Ask God** to help your congregation to worship in such a way that others are drawn to Jesus.
- **Ask God** to help you experience His desire for the worship of nations as you worship Him.
- **Ask God** to raise up worshipping evangelists who will go to the nations with worship as their main focus.

TAKE ACTION

Put a map of the world on a table or on a wall in your home. Use your favorite worship CD as you lay hands upon the nations and pray over them. Declare these Scriptures over the nations: "May the nations be glad and sing for joy, for you rule the peoples justly and guide the nations of the earth" (Psalm 67:4). "I will praise you, O LORD, among the nations; I will sing of you among the peoples" (Psalm 108:3).